Time for You, Butterfly

Time for You, Butterfly

Terra S. Garmon

FROM THE CORE

Copyright © 2022 by Terra S. Garmon, M.Ed. Printed in the United States of America. All rights reserved. Written permission must be secured from the publisher to use or reproduce any part of this book, except for brief quotations in critical reviews or articles.

Published by From the Core, LLC in Killeen, Texas. First Printing, 2022

Edited by Michelle L. Massie Early for ProEditor at www.proeditor.us.

From the Core, LLC books may be purchased in bulk for educational, business, fundraising, or sales promotional use. For information about purchases/services, please email, info@fromthecorellc.com.

Scripture quotation from Holy Bible, New Living Translation, copyright © 1996, 2004, 2015 by Tyndale House Foundation. Used by permission of Tyndale House Publishers, Inc., Carol Stream, Illinois 60188. All rights reserved.

ISBN: 978-1-7350847-4-9

Contents

Copyright iv
Dedication ix

Foreword 1

Preface 2

    I The Egg 4

Little Girl, little girl 5

Fun & Free 6

Shaping Me 7

Outlet for Life 8

I Don't Know? 9

My Soul to Keep 10

Shattered Perception 11

Without Spoken Words 12

Do Your Best to Trust 13

On a Temporary Visa 14

An Uncloudy Day 15

Roller Coaster	16
II The Feeding Stage	17
Expressions by Me	18
Pre-tend	19
Always a Dream	20
Taboo	21
Lost Moments	23
Broken Promises	24
Drives Me Mad	25
Will You Ever Speak My Language?	26
At Love's Speed	27
I Could've Loved You	28
Try Love	30
Love's Response	31
III The Transition	33
Midnight Hour	34
Peaceful Soul	35
Easy Saturday	36
Big Mommy	37
Uncommon	38
"32"	39
Song of the Pez	40

Surrender	41
Next, Please	42
Only You	43
In Secret	44
Time Changes	45
Everyday	46
Colors	47
Sweet Summer	48
IV The Adult Stage	49
Now, She Speaks	50
Up, Up, and Away	51
Just a Thought on Life	53
Last Century	55
A Keepsake	57
And So, It is Poetry	58
Kind of Love	59
Write it Loud	60
A Flash of Love	61
Endless Love	62
When We Are Touched	63
My Brothers	64
Freedom	65

Love	66
Red, Green and Black	67
Woman	69
DNA Not Forsaken	70
These 3 Words	71
In Privilege You Trust	72
Guilty	73
50!!!	74
City of Good Neighbors	75
The "One?"	76
Just Me & You	77
Destiny	78
Dark Chocolate, Please	79
Spring Breath	80
Love You	81
Contribute	82
Time for the Butterfly	83
Acknowledgments	84
About the Author	87

Dedicated to Mommy & Daddy.
When surrounded in LOVE, there is never an ending.

Foreword

Reading for me is like taking a trip. Each time I open a book, I know that my next adventure is about to begin. I am Terra's mother, born, reared, and educated in South Carolina. Working within the school system in the city of Buffalo, NY provided me with a sense of joy because I was able to create and develop young minds as we explored their imaginations. It was no surprise to me that my daughter, Terra, was interested in reading and eventually writing. Over the years, her writing has taken form in letters written to her family and within the work required to produce scholastic papers in college and graduate school.

No doubt her desire to express herself in writing stems from a personal motivation to put in print her ideas, thoughts, persuasions, hopes, and dreams that emulate her mind and heart. Thus inspired, Terra has completed this book of poetry dealing with the lives of the young, the older, and a myriad of natural and social phenomena. I hope you find encouragement and enlightenment as you read Terra's poetic expressions in this book.

Kitte J. Garmon
Mommy

Preface

I can still see the pink book with the word DIARY written across it in gold script and the metal clasp with a keyhole and tiny key to keep it safe and secure. I had this diary at a very young age and somehow knew then that writing was going to be instrumental in getting me through the turbulence and obstacles of life. As I write this, I wonder where that diary ended up. I don't remember discarding it, but I do remember how important it was to me at that time.

My mother had a large rose bush in our backyard that donned beautiful red roses. Those flowers often attracted butterflies. As I pause and reminisce, I remember the calm and gentle space I could bask in to escape the laborious and arduous thoughts that constantly bombarded my mind. It was during these quiet times I would write. I could say anything I wanted on those pages. There was no judgment, no disappointment, no correction – just an opportunity to be open and free.

It was always puzzling how everyone around me appeared to fit into this puzzle called life and that regardless of how I tried, I just never fit. I would think about my forever prince, the love of my life, coming to rescue me and tell me that all is well and that I will be ok. No matter how I may have wanted and wished for him to be, this was to no avail. However, it did not stop me from writing. It only made my passion and desire for LOVE even more compelling. This thought process carried me through college and into my adult years.

As I began forging ahead with my career and adult responsibilities, I did not dismiss love. I found an abundance of joy in writing about it, poetically expressing it, with an inward satisfaction that eventually I would understand it. Philadelphia and the tri-state area led me through a quandary of highs and lows. It brought me close to my family and gifted me with friends who are like family that I will always cherish. I discovered some of the most incredible and talented poets and spoken word artists. Their love of poetry was inspiring and allowed me to be alright with not only writing and creating but also sharing during open mic events. Those early times will never be forgotten.

Life is about seasons. It evolves, there are transitions, and there are periods when you may believe you have a better grasp than at other times. Continue to hold on. In this life, there will be constant learning, adapting, adjusting, *figuring out*, and change. The process remains. My focus in my teen and young adult years was centered around what I thought I needed in order to be extremely happy. As I have grown and matured, I have learned that this big ol' life is surrounded by what is unjust, inequitable, and unfair; and those woes matter to me now more than ever before. The strings of my heart have been *sprung* with this knowledge.

I want you to go through the transition and stages of life with an understanding that your darkest days do not have to keep you stalled, trapped, bound, and captured. As you read my selections, hold on tight to the belief that you will overcome whatever may be keeping you from showing up and presenting the best version of yourself. While continuously working through and in your process, you can and will spread your wings and fly. You will soar into your purpose and destiny. Do not give up, do not lose hope. You can choose your when, I say it is now, Time for You, Butterfly.

1
The Egg

"If an egg is broken by outside force, life ends. If broken by inside force, life begins. Great things always begin from inside."

Jim Kwik/Tamara Kulish

Little Girl, little girl

Little Girl, little girl why you wanna grow up so fast: before you know it, you'll look back and so many of your years will have passed.

Ponytails and high knee socks, uniforms and pleated skirts are a young girl's emblem in full stock.

Giggles, hopscotch, double-dutch, hide and go seek, a little girl's haven, still humble and meek.

Enticed by the media and all the glorious hype, trade your virginity for popularity and be accepted by all types.

Lie after lie, so loud and so clear, it is so hard to keep you protected because that's what you see and hear.

So Little Girl, little girl, take your time on destiny's pursuit before you even think to get involved with any of those name brands and cute hooded sweatsuits.

Close your legs, don't pop your gum, listen to your elders, they have a lot of wisdom.

Little Girl, little girl you will become older soon enough, then life will make you prove you're really strong, bold and tough.

But, until then Little Girl, little girl, won't you stay? Don't worry, you'll become a woman; you just keep living day after day.

Fun & Free

Pirouettes, jazzercise, yellow tutus and the song, *Ticket to Ride*, those years of practice and recitals brings a smile with a feeling of happiness and fulfillment.

Black leotards and off-white stockings preparing to move from flat ballet slippers into my hard-toed shoes, so I'd be ready for pointe.

Splits, forward and sideways, not fully flexible, but that didn't stop me from living out my dream of dancing wherever my little feet would land.

National Spelling Bees and Richmond Speaking Contests – repetition so I'd memorize words, lines of my next speech, and a character's role in a play.

These things were of a young girl, fun and free which continues to intrigue me. How did she lose herself, when in these moments she also found comfort, acceptance and peace?

Shaping Me

Surrounded by her thoughts in a world that only her dark room knew.

It was in those moments she would find the permission to just be herself.

Unsure, awkward, but with a smile that could set the world ablaze, too bad she found that out much later, for in her quiet moments she would cry, her mind spinning in a maze.

Her gaze pierced the depths of her hurting soul, wishing for assurance and confidence, instead drowning in pain after her heartache would take its toll.

The sadness overwhelmed her, so she hid all she felt. It was what she was accustomed to do. After all the denial she had become a pro, but in her room, she had nothing to prove.

Outlet for Life

My pen searches for what to say,
trying to make sense of all this disarray.
Thoughts, feelings, emotions all pushed away.
The ink on my paper is the only outlet left today.

I Don't Know?

If I can't tell the truth here, then where? I don't know.

If I can't express how I feel, then what?

If I can't tell you how deeply I hurt inside, then why?

If I can't be ME even on paper then it's all a lie.

If I can't open up and share what keeps me smiling for a long while, you say, "when will I be for real?"

When will I ever show my hurts, my pains, my triumphs and all of which I deal?

When will I take my thoughts from within and let you see what I've come to be?

For me it's been a long time laughing, hurting, crying, screaming, fighting, trying to get out from underneath.

You don't understand because you only wish to see just what you want, but not what is right in front of your face and because of that I constantly feel out of place.

So, I write to say what I need, there is no judgment, just my mind, paper, and pen.

Ask me only one time what's up, and for you, I'd let you in.

My Soul to Keep

Truth, but an illusion, often untold, lying beneath a cloud of dust, where deep within you can be seen, shaken, afraid, bewildered, and aware that this cloud by which you have staked your life must disappear.

Your freedom awaits you; the chains choke you and try to tear you down, but the darkness of your soul's journey keeps you awake.

The sounds of the dynamic currents and waves in your mind's eye sing of determination and truth that you, indeed, were always free.

So with deep breaths you sigh and ponder, imagine and wonder, could this Truth be yours too, free to be, who you were made to be?

Shattered Perception

The images are deceiving, one sees what they want.

A smile, a frown, a cry – it's all in the eyes of the one looking on.

If you shut them even for a second you might be fooled, your thoughts are bound to be shattered.

Your wants, your wishes, your desires, are they truly your own or are they created by those who hold the power?

Do you know if all is real, or is it a shattered perception?

Open your eyes wide, look hard, look long, search for the truth.

If you think you've got it, you probably do, so don't let it go.

It's hard to find again. After all, it's still a perception, not theirs, not mine, but yours.

Without Spoken Words

Bittersweet reality.

That's what it feels like when you finally understand

the uncertainties, the confusion around you.

Expressing one's self with words is hard, but rather you sit in

silence and let your actions speak for you.

You feel so distant, set apart, not quite like yourself.

Who knows how long this will last?

Maybe tomorrow you will feel differently, but I doubt it.

Do Your Best to Trust

So alone, so scared, so distant – that's what she feels.

Will the pain, the emptiness, ever go away?

So many people would like to enter her world, but why?

She doesn't know them, and they don't know her.

What are their intentions, what are their motives?

She's so unsure, so she keeps them outside, looking in,

that's where she feels it is most safe.

If they are special they will get to know her one day.

On a Temporary Visa

Someways from home

Someways far from home

I am someways from home

Far away from home

This earth is not my home

This earth is not my home

Far away from home

Heaven is my home

Heaven is my home

Where I'll find my eternal rest

Far away from home

Where I will be free at last

This earth is not my home.

An Uncloudy Day

The emptiness that is inside fills the mind. One wonders when it will go away. No one sees it as you do, so instead of crying you smile and wave.

The hurt that surrounds the soul is like an endless tunnel that goes on forever. One wonders if it will ever stop but it never does.

It can be unbearable, devastating, excruciating. Some are driven to the external forces that lead to the destruction of their own being. Others just die.

Would anything make a difference? A hug, maybe a kiss? But are they really enough? Even love, would that do it? Yes, but only, only, only, I believe, if it is the love of Jesus.

Roller Coaster

Twisting, unsettled, rolling around the mind

like a loose kite somewhere in the wind.

Will you even be able to catch it, grab it,

or is it just a figment of your imagination?

L O V E

11

The Feeding Stage

"Eat what nourishes your body. Do what nourishes your soul. Think what nourishes your mind."

Author Unknown

Expressions by Me

No more interruptions and carefully crafted words. Expressions by me should just flow naturally.

No more "What if I die, what would someone think about my thoughts left behind, would they wonder in dismay what was happening in my mind?"

It is no longer important how you may view me, because I got freed one day in June '06 at the October Gallery.

A tribute to the October Gallery in Old City Philadelphia

Pre-tend

the browns of your eyes, so truthful and unrelenting but still they disguise what you feel inside

we try the game of hide and seek but in just one round, game's over because you pre-tend that what we see is not even there

why do you deprive yourself of that one thing you have desired always? it's a game i can't play anymore because the taunting is endless

it becomes a mastermind of careful, strategic moves trying to unveil your next clue

you pre-tend to throw me off your track because somehow the unknown keeps the thrill of it all going

but this game of pre-tend doesn't work for me anymore because somewhere inside it got serious, intense way beneath my center's core

so, it is over, you've won, because all we've done is pre-tend that what we felt that day never existed

now neither of us has to say a word, back to the way it was and will always be

i guess in a sense we start the game of pre-tend all over because you pre-tend that what we see is not even there.

Always a Dream

I thought I smelled you on my pillow, though your head never laid there.

My thoughts quickly raced, for I wanted not to feel the way I did, because to others it would be viewed as wrong – not the right time.

My heart knew, for it never lies. Is all of this real? I pinched myself – no I'm not dreaming, I'm living.

Taboo

The trees sway as do my hips at the sound of your voice.

Mountains in the distance only emphasize what I want nearest to me.

The sweltering heat makes my insides yearn to be held by you.

The smell of the morning takes me to a familiar past.

Sunsets and the moon's presence beckoning to the night, increasing the thoughts of what I fear to talk about.

I lay quietly listening to my feelings trying to subdue what is so real about me.

The dawn appears and I make believe again that what is taboo never bothered me to begin with.

A quiet entrance as day breaks, an unresisted smile immediately is seen upon my face.

Another penetrating moment forces me to deal with me, what I want, what I must do.

In the wake of it all I just focus on being with you.

It is not possible, though my thoughts simplify it all and make it so easy.

What I've come to realize is that it passes and what is so far beyond me is really just a thought, and will never truly ever be for real.

As it passes across my mind, I leave it there.

It is taboo for a reason.

Lost Moments

Thoughts of you become the only focal point to me.

Monopolizing my time better spent carrying out various tasks throughout the day.

Thoughts of you resurrect that which I believed was dead inside.

Scares me over and over again for I can't seem to forget what it felt like to love and then to hurt.

Thoughts of you make me scream, "One more chance!" but there is none for us, we've already taken too many.

Broken Promises

You broke your promise to me

You broke your promise to me

You said we'd always be friends

You said you'd love me 'til the end.

You broke your promise to me

You broke your promise to me

Don't you care anymore about what you say,

the impact it has on others, your integrity?

Who can I trust now? Who should I believe?

If your words are nothing but empty, maybe theirs are too?

I have to believe that even though you broke your promise,

Maybe the next will do what they say?

I'm not sure, it's hard for me to travel this way again

But I promise, I will, one day.

Drives Me Mad

It is maddening that I didn't say all that I wanted to you on that night not long ago.

Scared of what I was feeling and unsure of what you would have thought.

Funny how time passes and things make better sense in my head, sometimes it is a bit too late – it was not you that needed convincing but me, instead.

I only have thoughts now to consume me, overwhelm me, or even delight me.

If only I could see you one last time, then all that is inside my mind would flow.

Caught up in the moment and the fluctuation of my heartbeats, I forgot to take it slow.

Who knows if we will ever meet again? In that one encounter, I learned so much.

Another time is not promised. Embrace the moment while it is there and make it count.

Until next time...or could it be never?

Will You Ever Speak My Language?

Will you ever speak my language? Similarly, specifically, softly, sincerely?

Will you ever speak my language? Genuinely, gently, gingerly?

Will you ever speak my language? Encourage me, support me, comfort me, hold me, defend me, protect me?

Will you ever speak my language? Cry at times, laugh most times, cry and laugh at the same time?

Will you ever speak my language? With wisdom, strength, and vision, lead our dreams and what seems impossible, believe is possible?

Will you ever speak my language? Listen, talk, listen, listen, listen, listen.

Will you ever speak my language? Peacefully, hoping in Thee, awaiting on Thee, trusting calling on Thee the Trinity, patiently and in faith with me?

Will you ever speak my language?

¡Hola! Cómo estás? Hello, I am well and you?

At Love's Speed

His velocity engulfed the night similar to the ocean's thrust against the shore's beginnings.

Unaware of the magnitude and force by which he imploded, that place that was barren, wanting, desiring, deserving respect but so much more.

Love anchoring his stance waiting to overtake his next victim laying quietly, awaiting his discovery.

His velocity engulfed the night, anxiously seeking to uncover treasures only imagined, time is with him, cautiously he investigates the surface.

Fearful of making any mistakes, meticulous calculations produce his next move.

Former experiences cannot guide him, only lead amiss.

Using a much less crafted, skilled technique. He blew through the night.

He re-centers, balances, heart, mind, body and soul because this one is a keeper, one that could keep his heart, protect his intentions, carry him to safety.

His velocity engulfed the night, not knowing what to do, he pauses, listens to the openness of the air, ponders the silence and expects an answer.

For this one, it's just the beginning.

I Could've Loved You

I could've loved you if my sun and your moon met just for a moment.

I could've loved you if my lyric and your rhyme connected in more than just poetic suggestions.

I could've loved you if rainbows had more than just slight, short-lived beauty.

I could've loved you.

I could've loved you if our spirits and souls agreed on the most important things.

I could've loved you when your confidence met my heart in laughter.

I could've loved you because of your innate ability to understand my beat without question.

I could've loved you. Maybe I should've loved you.

I could've loved you when your musical words capsulized my thoughts, my feelings.

I could've loved you if I were willing to lose, just this time in just this way, I know I could've loved you.

I could've loved you if you understood a hug for me can be a call to check in and speak me to sleep, oh yeah, I could've loved you.

I could've loved you if I believed in fairy tales, glass slippers, and gingerbread houses.

I could've loved you.

I could've loved you if I enjoyed the ride and didn't care about the destination.

I could've loved you.

I could've loved you, maybe I should've loved you, but I never loved you, 'cuz I wasn't supposed to love you, at least not that way and not in this lifetime.

Try Love

No one said you had to be brilliant, obtain your Master's, your Ph.D. or any of those things.

It can be a simple hello, a little smile, or just the wink of an eye.

Don't make it so difficult, so complex and so calculating. Let it be real and genuine, just let it happen.

Those who have it figured out should grab a hand and help someone else to understand it.

Stop using it to hurt, to control, and to kill.

Just allow it to be natural and free. Take it as it comes, don't try to push it away.

It can be very special and fulfilling, if you just give it a chance.

Love.

Love's Response

Confounding the hearts of many, capturing the feelings of most. Alluding those desiring, beseeching those afraid, what would love say?

Foolishly criticized by wants of a perfectly wrapped presentation. Numerous days, years, spent seeking ways to attain, materialize and sustain your presence.

Too beautiful to be juxtaposed somewhere. Too powerful to be exposed everywhere.

But you, so many want to know, what would you say? Webs woven together, the sprung too vulnerable for words but too affected to pretend you never existed.

The caveman, strongman, modern man, today's man no more educated about your bewildering effects, but all stand in humble adoration of your profound impact.

Still, the question remains, what would love say? Envisioning touching you becomes a priceless commodity.

One that oh so many are willing to kill for, die for and give anything for.

Dreams, visions, imagination, fantasies, captivate us, an audience never tired, always wondering, figuring, speculating about you, love, what would you say?

Fights, wars, arguments alike, abuse, violence to prove you despite.

You oh love, what would you say? Tears, separation, pain and fear, keep you away from many, but on the minds of most.

'Tis better to have loved, if it's meant to be, cliché upon cliché, just wait and see.

In the midst of struggling to find you, one asks, what would you say?

Then Love responds, I have always been here, if you open your mind, seek Me with your whole heart, it is then you will find Me.

III

The Transition

For everything there is a season, a time for every activity under heaven.

Ecclesiastes 3:1 (NLT)

Midnight Hour

Crickets, the moon glaring through your window – this is the midnight hour.

The sounds of late-goers racing through the streets, playing their late-night jams – this is the midnight hour.

A time of thought and meditation; trying to calm the mind down from all of the days' many events – this is the midnight hour.

So unsuspecting, yet an expectant air about it, almost to say something is going to happen, for it always does because this is the midnight hour.

Peaceful Soul

birds rappin' their favorite tune by my window in the wee morn

trees swayin' in the wind as spring becomes summer

the oceans pound on Hawaii's shore a sight to bestow

a day at the park watchin' the squirrels gleefully hunt for nuts

mint chocolate chip ice cream where the chips are undoubtedly chocolate and you feel the mint freshen you up

the moon waving goodbye as it cascades down my blinds makin' room for the glory of the sun

a baby's pure and innocent laugh not yet jaded by the world's touch

hangin' out with family on the holidays and bowling with friends on the weekend

being able to write freely on any given day

naps on a Sunday on my couch after church

quiet, stillness, oneness with My Lord

Easy Saturday

Sitting back, feet propped up on the couch.

A little jazz or soft music in the background.

An interesting book about nothing in particular.

Sweatpants, t-shirt, a pair of socks.

Conversation with an old friend.

Nothing too deep, this is an easy Saturday.

Everyone needs one of those; one of the best medicines ever.

Oh, how I long for those Saturdays.

Big Mommy

Your knees smelt of alcohol as I gently caressed all of the day's cares and demands away.

Sitting in your lap made our times together so cherished and dear. It was hard to say, "see you later," as I waited for our next special "you and me" time.

I lay next to you while we slept through the night. Oh, my Big Mommy being with you was more than just right.

Your smile and laugh I can remember crystal clear, how we sang *Precious Lord* for my mommy and my aunties to hear.

When I close my eyes and think of you, my heart reverberates and reminds me you are never far away.

Thankful for your sweet memory which stays with me every day.

Uncommon

What was the struggle all about? To be like everyone else? How senseless, how boring, how played out.

Didn't you know the careful design that was orchestrated when from clay you were made?

The thought and time to create you from the Omniscient mind.

How unthankful it seems to be when we spend so much effort and money to wear, think, talk and express like those on TV.

Unique, different, yes, a rarity, no two exactly alike because that would be dull, unattractive, predictable, and common.

So, rise to the occasion. You are exactly who you were meant to be, no mistakes, no afterthoughts, nothing common here. You, after all, are very uncommon.

"32"

32 was me and you

constant rhythmic music playing in the background

playful banter back and forth

promises of a future too

books, candles, neatly packaged

glances over sweats and tired feet

only to be understood through our next meet

innuendos softly spoken over lunch breaks

long conversations with nothing at stake

regrets, none here, oh, I'm so glad we met that year

and even though 32 will never be

you will always remain with me...

Song of the Pez

I can't exactly remember the number of days that we talked but I think it was a year.

You were clear about your intentions and that you wanted me to be yours, close by, near.

We would laugh and discuss everything. I didn't want anything more than what we had.

Simple glances, the easiness that we felt there was just a natural way in which we communicated.

Never forced, no pressure, just two young adults, just friends.

I didn't know that over that year, my heart had begun to really enjoy you.

I didn't know that who I declared as just my friend, was beginning to become something more.

My heart went on an exploration – it wanted to be loved.

It no longer needed my permission it knew where to go to heal my inner cry.

Without warning, you swam right where you knew you would be nourished, treasured, and held.

It was at that moment that the mystery of love was discovered and unveiled.

Surrender

Perspiration falls like raindrops down the side of a window.

It excites you.

The thumps of your heart sound like the drummer boy from afar.

Satisfaction beyond anything ever known before.

This pleases you.

Like loose ends that are finally tied together, you feel as though you've met your match.

It scares you, so you take your time.

But until that moment, you only surrender small pieces of yourself.

Just enough for that day, more will be given tomorrow.

Next, Please

I keep asking myself, what are you doing? I don't get it, nor do you.

You say you want us, then you don't act, moving mysteriously like a black cat.

Into the dark my mind wanders, looking, longing, wishing for you. You don't come, so why don't I just let go?

While my fingers cling to the cliff before I fall, I keep asking myself, are you worth it at all?

Mostly I am good, Bus 18 and our shared moments many moons ago, won't let me stop spinning in my head.

I am tired and expectations of you only bring dread.

The idea that you could possibly think we have a lifetime to go, your movement only shows you have no ideas, no plans, for you move way too slow.

I know what to do so I remember to be strong and I will show you.

Love and love and love but your love always seemed greater…but I may never know until I see My Lord the Creator.

Only You

Your touch becomes your word of comfort; the sign that irrespective of what is happening, we will be more than okay.

It is in that special place I remember how it was, what made me smile, what made me stay and what made us overlook some of the nuances and mistakes.

Your touch gave permission for the essence of which I am defined to be revealed because of that I will never be the same.

What we have shared, ultimately, is without shame.

In Secret

Secrets they kept, thinking it was for the good, only to learn that operating in that vein can make even the innocent misunderstood.

What is the purpose for walking that way? Oh, to hold onto pride, while perpetuating untruths and lies.

Silence, mind your own business, is what we were always told.

This keeps you out of the fire, the muck and vicious fold.

Too hard of a line to keep straight, so set the parameters, be gentle, correct, but never berate.

Stop living a secret life. It is easier to maintain when you are free from guilt, shame, and strife.

Keep your mouth off of others and work to keep all that you have as together as can be.

For should your tomorrow come, you will see, it is much easier to focus all of your attention on you and not me.

Time Changes

It's crazy how time flies, one minute you are young and the next you are looking around at all of the precious memories made.

Stay present is what you choose, staying in the past has proven, there is much to lose.

You hear a song and it quickly reminds you of another time, sometimes simpler, sometimes not.

As time changes you've come to understand life and how we have been given a certain lot.

The thankfulness that erupts within you tells you that you are steady, not exasperated, nor anxious, or confused but patient and yes, oh so very present.

Time is different now, how you see it, how you treat it. Remain true, you Remain you too.

Time changes.

Everyday

Everyday I work, then I rest and work some more. I enjoy my nights and even a few days when I can sit and just relax some more.

Everyday I pay my bills and then pay them some more. Come home, sit down for barely a second, get the kids off to bed and work some more.

Everyday on the phone trying to do what I can to make all my ends meet, by the time I'm done it feels like major defeat.

For Everyday comes and I do this some more, waiting for my change, this stuff to change some more. Can this be all that my life was meant for? To grind and hustle and do it some more?

No, I have to believe that there is so much more. I have to look to create and make it be more. Everyday does seem like I'm doing the same thing I've been doing, but more and more.

Written for all the hard-working people who are waiting for their "American dream" to be realized.

Colors

Looking out at the trees your visitation always makes me smile,

the blues, the reds, are never overwhelming

it almost feels as though you do not see how special you are.

You are a welcoming surprise and you never disappoint.

As you await the arrival of a friend, you sing and sing

carefree as ever and never moved by your surroundings.

Oh, to always be free and remember peace is mine.

I look at you and you remind me to be still, you remind me of freedom, you remind me not to worry, and you remind me that Love is ever-present.

I will never tire of seeing you.

Sweet Summer

Ah, sweet summer, won't you stay?

Where will the crickets sound, where will they play?

Ocean waves, children splashing, how fast it all dissipates, the memories start flashing.

Mosquitoes, green grass, flowers all abloom, best sherbet in town, September is upon me, summer will be gone too soon.

This is how it ebbs and flows, the change of seasons.

Remain stagnant if you choose, but what would be your reason?

New birth, new smells, new life, a changing earth, embrace the seasons, view them for what they are worth.

Nothing remains the same, this life is a journey, walk slow or fast, day by day it will surely pass.

Summer is fading and will be gone, but as I live it will be back upon me very soon.

IV

The Adult Stage

> "My humanity is bound up in yours, for we can only be human together."
>
> Desmond Tutu

Now, She Speaks

Like a raindrop that becomes an immediate part of the surface below, so too are your words, your glances, and your thoughts.

But every day unfolds the start of a blossoming flower that has overcome the trials and tests that were placed to defeat it.

A butterfly free from its cocoon, a bird not entangled by any foes below, or a hunter's gaming sport laid out for its capture.

So too is she that chooses liberty and her voice. Too often quieted by the increasing sounds around her and the fear within.

She has escaped and is walking day by day, breath flowing with less effort.

Her choice now is to be heard, not swallowed up by the surface below, but erupting with great force and great power.

Can you hear her?

Up, Up, and Away

the birds are free they flap their wings

and fly from place to place in search of

comfort to care for their needs.

I, much like a bird, have flown

searching for that

special place where I could rest, and let

open my wings.

where I looked there was no peace, no

solace, so I kept flying until

I could not fly anymore.

one of my wings had become

limp. I looked around and all I saw was

the ground below me.

my remaining wing could not do it

alone, so for a moment

I thought I'd just stop flying.

but Someone within me, told me no,

I will not let you go.

so, He told me to keep flying.

I was not tired any longer,

both my wings were brand new.

I was not searching for that peace or comfort

for I know I have peace and comfort in Him.

I was not sure where I was going but

with Him leading, I would be okay.

He told me He would never lead me astray.

so, I kept flying, with Jesus as my guide.

Just a Thought on Life

Sometimes life doesn't work out the way you want it.

You have a picture in your mind of how it's all goin' down and most times that picture is never developed.

It's not for you to become weary, distant, or unconnected...but to show you that there is Some-One with a greater plan than you could ever imagine.

Allow the quiet moments of your life to shape you, create you, and make you.

Learn to accept your role, your place, your position in this life.

It will do you good to relax more, not worry so much, and just be cool with the day-by-day.

Definitely challenge, pursue, fulfill destiny and remember that destiny lies within you, but you need the One to bring it out.

Don't shrug your shoulders and act like you don't know because you can feel it, sense it, and almost touch it.

It's yours, go after it, you won't have to do it alone. Let the Lord take you where you've never been, open your heart, uncover what's been hidden, and allow your light to shine.

This is life, you only have to follow the Way before you. So walk carefully, wisely, and purposefully. You will be there sooner than you know, and what a peaceful place that will be.

Last Century

Sacred are the days long gone by, youthful pleasures, impulsive dares, safety assured, parents prepared, guarding their children from the enemy's snare.

Hellos and thank you's, a thing of the past, replaced with arrogance, rudeness, and you can talk to the hand.

No, I don't understand how we can disregard one another, all for the sake of the mighty dollar? Pimping, politicking, masquerading behind the cares of the people? Meanwhile, perpetuating killings of those same people? Spreading lies to fight and bring down the "evil power" when you know behind closed doors you've sat and dined with this same power?

Where are the days when your word really was bond and in your eyes was the truth, not lies? Don't get me wrong. We all suffer from some of the same frailties, after all, we are all human, but what about the honest desire to get things right, respect one another, forgive, or is peace a forgotten plight?

So sacred are the days that have gone by, walking down the street, money not strapped down against your chest, looking behind your back for help so you can rest and not because you are afraid of getting robbed or attacked.

Those days seem to allude us now, in this age of "I-ism" and "Me-ism" which all boils down to "Selfish-ism." There used to be a time when we would help someone else out of a sense of reward and fulfillment from just being nice, not because we were looking to get paid.

Sacred are the days long gone by, youthful pleasures...I miss you.

A Keepsake

An undaunting collection of wisdom carefully packaged

The answer to the perplexing question that weighed so heavily on my brain

Undiscovered places, far away, never done justice through the camera's lens

A rose, each layer carefully opened to showcase its beauty once more

Passion for love, all its intensity, savored for the right person

The perfect movie that plays over and over in your mind

A memory that causes laughter at any given moment

And So, It is Poetry

Like a cool glass of water after a long run

so is my poetry

Like a hug after being told some devastating news

so is my poetry

Like a piece of cornbread with sweet potato pie so

is my poetry

Like laughter after the night's funniest comedian

so is my poetry

Like a warm wool coat in 20-degree weather

so is my poetry

Like a kiss from someone dear

so is my poetry

Like a beach on a tropical island

so is my poetry

Like seeing you every day and every night

so is my poetry

Like being able to love you always so is my poetry

(love is poetry)

Kind of Love

I want the kind of love that makes you hold hands when you're 80, you don't care about the sleep in my eyes kind of love or the body changes I'll go through kind of love.

You're sad when I'm sad and happy when I'm happy because we're in this together kind of love.

The kind of love you see in the movies where you fly across the ocean and don't give up so easily kind of love, or there's nothing I can do to make you stop lovin' me kind of love.

The kind of love where we stare at trees and climb up mountains and travel all around the world kind of love, where we can pop some popcorn kind of love. The kind of love where your deepest treasures are where you placed the key to my heart. Where you've locked away my secrets kind of love.

Seeing a thunderstorm ahead and providing the right protection instead kind of love.

I don't have to worry because when you say you got it you do kind of love...that's open and honest, rarely seen, seldom achieved, dreams are made of kind of love, free and inspiring, motivating and never tiring, that's the kind of love I want...how 'bout you?

Write it Loud

With my pen I write about the endless fight for peace, for justice, for love, and so much more.

Able to say exactly the right words in the right way, make my point.

With my pen I write, stop the fighting, pray for peace and justice for all.

With my pen I write that no person, nor community should be

devalued and made to feel worthless and small.

With my pen I will continue to write until there is nothing more to say.

With my pen I write, freedom is for me and you. Shouldn't that be the nation's way?

A Flash of Love

The colors flash across my mind, reminding me of the endless ways in which you love me.

With a fierce energy and desire that is strong, your touch tells me I am yours and you are mine.

At times, I forget what was once so easy, only to quickly be revived through your smile, your way, and the softness of your style.

Love is here and yet gone tomorrow so it would appear.

I close my eyes and I think, I choose to remember that real love is never gone, never wasted, never forgotten.

A love so pure, unashamedly potent is one to be cherished and never forsaken.

Endless Love

Endless love is for real, I know it to be the true deal.

No matter what has happened in my life, our first touch, a major decision, boy it was so much.

Who knew that what we knew to be our day-to-day would change in such an immense way?

I ponder over those earlier times and think, what if I had kept my secret place solely as mine?

When and who would we be? Had I protected me and stayed away from the intimacy.

Love like this though I would have never known, and the power to love with such fierceness was and still is our own.

Endless love, yes, it is for real. You and I both know it is the real deal.

When We Are Touched

So many people travel through life feeling unloved, unwanted, yearning to be touched.

Those same people hurt themselves trying to please everyone for that feeling of love, or just a touch.

It is so hard to understand why we don't express ourselves more, tell someone they are loved, and that their existence has been a blessing for us, we have been touched.

Surely someone has made you smile, changed your life in just a blink of an eye.

Find that someone and let them know what it is they've done. Don't wait 'til they are no more, tell them now while you have the chance.

Tell them they are loved and that you have been touched.

My Brothers

Brothers, brothers, everywhere, do I dare stare?

Brown brothers, ebony brothers, fair-skinned, olive brothers.

Brothers, brothers, everywhere, do I dare stare?

Tall brothers, short brothers, thin brothers, thick brothers.

Brothers, brothers everywhere, do I dare stare?

Strong brothers, working brothers, "need a little help" brothers, Educated by the system or the streets brothers.

Brothers, brothers everywhere, do I dare stare?

Dreadlock brothers, "baldy" brothers, cutey brothers, fine brothers, Smart brothers, "got a good sense of humor" brothers, witty brothers. Brothers, brothers everywhere, do I dare stare?

Romantic brothers, charming brothers, sensitive brothers, "he's so nice" and I just wanna be friends brothers.

Whoever you are, I pay respect to you. Brothers, brothers, everywhere. Would you mind if I took a second stare?

Freedom

Freedom calls from the mountaintop but I can't hear it.
Like a mighty rushing wind it howls, creating an aftermath within my soul.
Erupting emotions of shame and pain, fear and doubt.

Tormenting tornadoes cloud my judgment, causing self-hatred to flood in like torrential downpours.

Freedom demands my attention but I can't hear it.

Like an illuminating light troubling my heart, it has signaled for Triple A – ask, answer, accept.

Rainy days are here again, but then I remember joy comes in the morning when I rise, freedom can part its wings and fly, for no longer does freedom call from the mountaintop;

The sun bows to the moon no more, removing last night's tidal wave of guilt and insecurity.
Freedom is calling how I hear it, like a still small voice, I can receive it.
Freedom is calling, don't you hear FREEDOM calling you?
Don't you hear freedom calling you? Jesus, don't you hear freedom calling you, Jesus.
Written for those still trying to find their way.

Love

Love, I think I finally see you. Not all glitter and gold, butterflies and eagerness.

Love, you are a constant stream of flowing nutrients that supports and cares beyond all odds and any obstacle.

Love, you are the dying breath that decides to save a life instead of your own, take a shot to maintain your truth.

Love, you remind me that I am securely yours and never will I lose you.

Love, I believe I really know you now, a lifetime of regrets and disappointments have shown me you.

You, love, never let me down, you lift and encourage and tell the truth irrespective of who is around.

You, oh love, are not about giddiness and laughter and the ever-changing fleeting heart of emotions.

You are reverent, stable, unmovable, and patient.

Love, you never wonder where I am because you are sure to remain with me always.

Oh, how my discovery of true love has freed my soul, now I too can love like you.
Invested and faithful, dedicated and reliable, loyal and just here, always.
How I love, LOVE.

Red, Green and Black

Red, green and black reminds me of my Ancestors' trek, from a land where gold, pyramids, purple and royalty was not entertainment for the imagination but a reality manifested naturally.

Red, green and black reminds me of my connections to a proud people, in-charge people, never beaten people but determined people to share one another's dreams people.

Red, green and black reminds me of unity, solidarity and collective responsibility, together we can make it.

Red, green and black hollers strength, innovation, invention, determination and motivation.

Red, green and black echoes the sounds of drums, perpetual, uninhibited, clapping, dancing, singing praises to the Lord and all of heaven.

Red, green and black; red, green and black; red, green and black reminds me of the deepest seas, uncharted waters, rainbows of colors rarely experienced, the red, the green and the black.

Red, green and black reminds me of my connections to a proud people, in-charge people, never beaten people but determined people, to share one another's dreams people.

Red, green and black reminds me of generation after generation of hard workers, disciplined, focused, strong leaders, powerful leaders, influential leaders, can affect change leaders.

Red, green and black signifies Fatherhood, Motherhood and we are all family hood.

Red, green and black reminds me of my home, never stolen from me, never taken from me.

Red, green and black not only reminds me of me but red, green and black is me.

Woman

In charge, large, boisterous woman, beaten down, encouraged, strengthened woman. Big voice, little voice, no voice, unheard woman. Always having to fight for your rights, it comes easy for you woman.

Don't mess with my kids, these are my babies, and yes barren woman. Married, single, divorced, widowed woman. Up, down, happy, sad, you can take it all but then you can't woman.

Intense, giggly, scared, shy, flirtatious woman. Sing, sing a song, out loud and strong woman, hear me roar, wild woman, "put my foot in it" cooking woman, now I'm a career woman.

Sexy, frumpy, tomboy, high heels, wedges, flip flops, my feet hurt woman. Playful, serious, "let's kick it," keep a secret, gossiper, rapping woman, what I'm saying is, excuse me, woman. Neck, eye-rolling, cantankerous woman, "ooo you so evil" woman.

Cry all the time, can't cry at all woman, if I ruled the world, homemaker woman, proud, abused, embarrassed woman. I don't care, so what, no, don't leave me, woman.

Light, dark, small, average size, healthy woman. Complex, smart, simple, and maybe even not-so-bright woman.

But Woman, Woman, Woman, whoever you are, Woman. God created Woman and declared you are beautiful, Woman.

DNA Not Forsaken

Ancestry – the traces on my face though some hews are dark, some lighter, but the effects are apparent of this race. To have walked with the giants of times past, whether you did or not, how can you not be touched by what they stood for, lived for, died for so you could have more.

I did not know them but their impact is felt as I walk freely through the streets, talking to this one and that one without the overwhelming need to hide or retreat.

My dreams, my dreams show me life with you, pleasantries exchanged, the royalty held – King/Queen you still are even though you let them rob your heritage with the lies they've told that keep you behind *mental* bars.

I see so clearly that which you possess so how can you not be touched, you are them; they are you, a union that can't be broken, for my ancestry – the traces on my face some hews are dark, some lighter, but it is apparent, I have been affected by this race.

These 3 Words

Reliable, indescribable, undeniable,

Loyal, trustworthy, dependable,

Caring, compassionate, infinite

Remarkable, breathtaking, patient

Witty, smart, confident

Faithful, honest, thankful Visionary,

strong, giver Appreciative, creative,

demonstrative, So many words

To describe this

Thinking too hard

Don't miss it

Open your heart

Please know this

You tell me

I'll tell you…

I LOVE you.

In Privilege You Trust

You act like you enforce an honest statute but those of us who've been around know the truth. Trying to tell me that my freedom and yours is the same, who's kidding who?

You won't speak up when rights are violated and think a hand on the heart will cause me to ignore your part. My country and sweet land of injustice and you sing liberty for a few with the right hue (according to you).

No matter how many lives lost, you fight to be right, refuse to denounce in more than just words, deplorable acts alike, you focus on keeping the "green" in your pocket and your businesses afloat. Forget about the shame, all you do is stare and gloat.

Greed and pride riding your back with taunting and bullying you launch your attack.

You've never had to suffer unfair practices, lack of opportunities allude your view.

When you close your eyes what do you see? I hope to be wrong but I envision you saying, yes, it's all about me, me, me.

Responding, reacting, and living "in privilege I trust" as do you, is not a possibility for me.

Throughout this life, I must and will continue to stand tall and firm in the face of adversity.

Guilty

They see us and they don't care

Just another one of THEM and they stare.

They try to intimidate, threaten and if we are

not scared they enjoy beating us, whipping us,

tasering us, pepper spraying us and YES even killing us.

No sweet way to look at it, no more benefit of the doubt.

It's all very clear, black and brown they fear.

Hands up, doesn't matter, fleeing the scene is worse,

so what if shot in the back or a knee to the throat for

9 minutes and 29 seconds. Human life may affect their

consciousness but for them a dog, a cat is more important

than the fact that we bleed the same blood. Don't know if

it will ever change but you know I am just fed up with the

silence. What you do is wrong and that is it, case closed.

You are guilty!

50!!!

Fifty, how peace now comes to me swiftly.

Free, being myself, not consumed by other's opinions as much.

Exploring interests, dreams made long ago, praying to fulfill my heart's echo.

Releasing, trusting my Lord's plan, watching it all unfold as it happens.

Doubts, insecurities in the distance where they will decay, overcome by purpose, faith, and clear direction.

50 is here, it would appear, faster than I imagined or thought in its time, as it ought.

50 free, 50 at peace, constant struggles have ceased.

City of Good Neighbors

I shall never apologize for the way the sun kisses my skin

Or the reverent way in which my hair stands to salute each day

The gallant trots and confidence with which I walk

Or the glances and stares I receive by the way I talk

My eyes, my nose, my stature, and athletic build

will never apologize if in my presence you become even smaller still

It is your corrupted mind that goes out seeking to harm

and your lack of confidence and insecurities

that provoke you and cause you great distress and alarm

For a moment we fell and in deep sadness we travailed

but believe this truth it is these defining moments when we rise again only to prevail.

Written for my beautiful city of Buffalo

The "One?"

It doesn't have to be just what they said, love is much different than what I've seen or read.

Wisdom always tells the truth, whether it is respected is the issue that keeps one aloof.

The constant, consistent, stable understanding that is known and felt creates a security, and loyalty that makes even the hardest of hearts melt.

Should you only walk by someone else's ideas or thoughts? It is only you in the end that will know if what you have molded was or is worth all you may have fought.

When all is said and done you have to know if this is the "one."

Just Me & You

Just me & you holding hands walking down the street without a care in the world. I feel you & you feel me.

Simple pleasures we both appreciate; the silences only stimulate.

What we have cannot be duplicated, comes around only once it was involuntarily created.

Just thinking of you sends smiles and thrills through my body. I wish there were more that knew what I know about this...but too much of you destroys the sacredness.

There are days when I ponder over the goodness we've shared, there is no one like you to compare.

Keep doing the things you do. I will always love you.

Destiny

I excitedly anticipate the thrill of the unexpected

Just thinking and writing about it makes the

exhalation of each of my breaths increase

while it intensifies my heartbeats.

So much anticipation for what is to come

A smile is pronounced on my face

Wondering, imagining, enjoying

This new place.

Overcome with delight

I close my eyes and everything feels right

The suspense just makes me want more

A glimpse here and there tells me what is in store.

Dark Chocolate, Please

A beautifully wrapped delicious piece of dark chocolate

Becomes my afternoon and evening treat

Just enough to take away the unyielding desire for something sweet

Melting, so slightly with the touch of my fingers

After eating just one, the want for more continues to linger

I ingest one more, with a lack of satiety that refuses to let me rest

I decide one more is all that I need, so with intention and specificity, I

consciously devour the last, it's dark chocolate I love, for I know it the best.

Spring Breath

In my backyard I sit, with the sun and shade hitting the earth balancing the atmospheric shift.

The birds chirp, while my evergreen, today, shows off a slight sway.

Children, adults, speaking across nature's bountiful voice, showing reverent display for this year's spring season.

Green grass, acres of land, a farmer's most happy space, crabs and fishing, folks aligned all over the place.

The water, ten minutes away, walk, bike, drive, all in just a few moments.

Spring is here, full of colors, sun, and rain.

I appreciate you now, more than ever.

Love You

Love you forever.

Love you no matter.

Love you, sweet darling.

Love you always.

Love you in the morning sun.

Love you whether right or wrong.

Love you, sweet darling.

Love you, my love.

Love you, my love.

Love you…

Contribute

What will you leave behind to contribute to this world, a legacy, an inheritance, or wisdom made of pearls?

And who will listen to your life's song and dance, did you say something lasting, significant or will you forfeit your last chance?

What message will you want to leave with those you leave behind? Knowledge, power, wisdom, and strength? Or will you fail to contribute anything at all?

What message will you want to leave with those you leave behind?

Think about it...

Time for the Butterfly

Escaped the tests of Time, managing to revive colors that once lay dormant within.

None could see as deep as you could, it was your sight that kept you ascending.

Swirling, turning and wrestling pushed you past a silken case that once weighed you down.

Closing in, destined to be you, endless searching became a vision for all to see.

Could the constant fear and doubt have kept you from becoming what you truly are?

It is a distant thought now because you are reborn.

Embrace. Envelop. Discover and transcend through this Time.

This Time will never be this way again.

So, it's Time for you, Butterfly.

---

* Also published in Ely H. *A Surrender to the Moon*. International Library of Poetry; 2005

Acknowledgments

Thank You, Jesus, my Lord and Savior!!! I love You with all my heart. There is no me without You. Thank You for Your faithfulness, your unfailing love, and for being the Lifter of my head. Lord, You receive all the glory, honor, and praise, because all of it belongs to You!!! Thank you for allowing this book to come to fruition and for continuing to fulfill the desires of my heart according to Your good pleasure. Lord, You have brought me to this place and I am forever thankful to You.

Mommy (Kittie) & Daddy (Gentre), I am so thankful that a Tennessean met a South Carolinian and he decided to pop the question and they decided to tie the knot over 56 years ago. You two always show up for me and remain constant. Thank you for your unwavering love and support. You're the best parents ever!!! Daddy, thank you for demonstrating what faithfulness to the Lord looks like and Mommy, for being a truly compassionate and caring soul. Through your example, I know that the Lord cares for me.

Danielle, my dear, sweet sister, your smile makes my entire world much better!!! Your requests for me when I am not with you remind me that I am missed and cared for in this life. Thank you.

Gentre, thank you, my brother, for all of our childhood play times, special language, *free-styling*, laughter, and jokes that only you and I get. Thank you, my sister-in-law, Dabralis. You and my brother have created a beautiful family and given me Dora, my niece/Goddaughter, and Nano, my nephew. Your children make my heart so very full and my face hurt from smiling. Thank you.

My grandparents, aunties, uncles, and all of my cousins, thank you for the love shown to me throughout my life.

Thank you to my Godchildren for bringing me so much joy. It is truly my delight to be your Godmommy.

My loved ones that have transitioned, I remember you and am thankful for the impact and the roles you all played in my life. I am reminded of your words and will cherish our times forever.

My loyal friend, Paul, thank you for reading through this and giving me the nod of encouragement to go ahead and publish. Thank you for your honesty, consistency, reliability, dependability, and solid advice. Regardless of any circumstances, you trust the Lord!!! Thank you for your constant example of a Jesus-filled life. You are truly a good friend and indeed a brother to me.

Cathie, thank you for reading this work and saying do it bestie-bb!!! Thank you for your continuous support, standing with me, and remaining true to our friendship and sisterhood. You are my bestie-bb!!!

Dr. Sheree, so thankful for that piece of lint in the hair that day!!! You have been such an inspiration in getting this work published. Your encouragement and Sheree-isms make the difference. Thank you, my friend and sister.

Artist extraordinaire, Kimberly, my friend. Thank you for graciously sharing your extensive knowledge of art and for your strong desire to make original art available to everyone. Thank you for the invitation to come to your gallery and present my poetry. Your artistic gifts have enriched my life and remain that quiet push to keep the creative parts of me alive!!!

Nanzetta, my friend and sister, when I call you, you are here. I appreciate the blend of friendship and family that you provide. Thank you.

Melissa, thank you my friend for our good college years, our sister-to-sister talks, all the wonderful memories, laughter, and for my NY family!!!

Emart, my lil'bro, thank you for your friendship and for showing up for me as you do.

To all of my friends, near and far, you hold such an important place in my life. Thank you for not allowing life's challenges, distance, or time to take over and create space between us. I am so thankful for each of you.

To the Philly poets and spoken word artists…y'all are AMAZING…open mics, venues, and every event I have attended…thank you for always welcoming me!!!

Finally, my Publisher, From the Core, editor, and the entire team, thank you for believing in this project and getting it ready for the world to see. I will always be thankful for your support and belief in this book.

About the Author

Terra S. Garmon was born and raised in Buffalo, NY. She has a Master of Education degree in Advanced Studies majoring in Social Science with a focus on Instructional Leadership. Terra is also certified as a Mind Body Fitness Coach. At a very young age, her desire was to help people. Her life's work is a reflection of that calling.

Terra enjoys her free time traveling, sitting by the ocean, being out in nature, riding her bike, collecting art, practicing yoga, spending time with family and friends, reading, singing at church, journaling, and being an avid "enjoyer" of all things jewelry.

Photo By: B'Captured Productions

www.ingramcontent.com/pod-product-compliance
Lightning Source LLC
Chambersburg PA
CBHW061730070526
44583CB00024B/3081